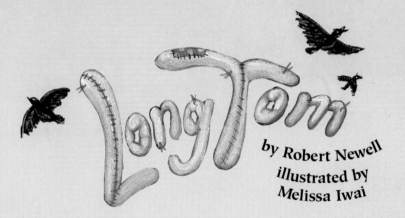

Long Tom

by Robert Newell

illustrated by
Melissa Iwai

Scott Foresman

Editorial Offices: Glenview, Illinois • New York, New York
Sales Offices: Reading, Massachusetts • Duluth, Georgia
Glenview, Illinois • Carrollton, Texas • Menlo Park, California

Long Tom had to watch the corn.
Pretty soon he saw something.

The cows were in the corn!

Long Tom had to do something.
Flap, flap, flap!

Away they went.

Long Tom saw something.

The raccoons were in the corn!

Long Tom had to do something.

Flap, flap, flap!

Away they went.

The crows were in the corn!

Long Tom had to do something.

Flap, flap, flap!

Away they went.

No one was in the corn.
There was no one to watch.

Flap, flap.

Long Tom was all alone.

"Come back!" he called.

The cows came back.

The raccoons came back.

The crows came back.

Then flap, flap, flap!
Away they went!